INNER PEACE & HAPPINESS

Reflections to Grow Your Soul

Inspirational poetry by

RICHARD JAFFE

Inner Peace and Happiness

What others are saying about this book:

"What other people may find in poetry or an art museum, I have found in the flight of a good drive. Yet, in this book, *Inner Peace and Happiness* by Richard Jaffe, you will find inspiration akin to what I've experienced on the course. I highly recommend it."

~ Arnold Palmer, American Golf Legend and member, World Golf Hall of Fame

"It's unusual and refreshing to find a successful businessman and philanthropist who writes inspirational poetry about love. Yet Richard Jaffe is that rare leader who helps us remember that love of our mission, family, colleagues, customers and friends is the essence of leadership."

~ Ken Blanchard, co-author of *The One Minute Manager®* and *Leading at a Higher Level*

"Richard's poetry breathes life into the words friendship, love and happiness. His poems serve as a constant reminder of what is important in life."

~ Gary Heil, co-Author of *One Size Fits One* and *Maslow On Management*

"'Words that come from the heart, enter the heart,' an old Hebrew proverb teaches. This is the case with Richard Jaffe's poetry, filled with vivid, emotionally compelling images. *Inner Peace and Happiness* is the heartfelt writing of a poet with a large, all-embracing heart."

~ Rabbi Joseph Telushkin, author of *A Code of Jewish Ethics,* and *Jewish Literacy.*

"Knowing Richard Jaffe as well as I do, I can tell you that he lives "The Secret" every day and his poetry reflects this timeless philosophy. Richards's unique ability to express his emotions so eloquently is sure to enamor his readers as each of his poems have captivated me."

~ Lisa Nichols, co-author of *Chicken Soup for The African American Soul* and *The Secret*

Inner Peace and Happiness

Reflections to Grow Your Soul

Richard Jaffe

Theresa,

As you travel along on the journey of life, may you always be blessed with Inner Peace and Happiness.

Love,

Richard

RBJ

ISBN-10: 0-9796234-0-5

ISBN- 13:978-0-9796234-0-0

Library of Congress Cataloging-in-Publication Data

Inner Peace and Happiness: Reflections To Grow Your Soul/Richard Jaffe

Cover Design by George Foster

Interior Design by Jessica Marony and Steve Bennett

Printed in the United States of America

10 9 8 7 6 5 4 3 2 1

Dedication

I am a very lucky man, lucky because I have experienced the life-changing effects of love. The poems in this book are expressions of emotions for the people I've loved, those who have loved me and the relationships and friendships that I treasure deeply. Most importantly, this book reflects the power of love.

Love has contributed greatly to my happiness and success as a businessman, philanthropist and author. It is quite impossible for me to acknowledge and to thank all of the people who've touched me in heartfelt ways. Since I am limited in space, I've focused on acknowledging the people who have been a core part of the journey that resulted in this collection of poems.

My wife Ann is my soul mate and best friend. She has taught me about compassion, consideration and generosity by the way she lives each day. She has brought great joy and inspiration to my life and many of the poems were written for her. Our son Brett, and daughters Charly and Maxi, are awesome and the great loves of my life. They are mirrors to my own soul and fill my life with pride and inspiration. My love for them is expressed in several of the poems found in this book. My parents, Irving and Eleanor Jaffe, taught me at an early age the importance of becoming a loving and giving person. Their caring touch and expression of affection while I grew up built the confidence and foundation for my own inner peace and happiness. My sisters, Joyce and Susan, and brother Jack, have taught me so much about unconditional love and sharing lifetime friendships. My cousin, Idonna, whose sense of humor and friendship I treasure more than words can express, has always been at my side, through life's ups and downs.

A philosopher once said that if a man has one true friend he is very blessed. I count myself exceedingly blessed for I have several friends who have made my life a much richer one. I thank each of you (you know who you are) who have shared my love and inspired both my poems and my life. You have taught me to make time every day to love, to laugh and to hug!

Finally, no project ever comes together well, whether it's a business or a book, without people behind the scenes contributing their talent. This book is no exception. I'd like to thank my dedicated team. Erin Marsh for her infectious positive attitude and for helping schedule my time and making sure that every detail is attended to. George Foster for creating a wonderful cover for this book and capturing its spirit. Deborah Stephens, who believed in me, helped me start my publishing journey and was the quarterback directing all my teammates. Gary Heil for encouraging me to finally publish and for being a true friend and a coach throughout the process. Steve Bennett for helping me capture today's technology to share my poems and thinking with others. Ken Druck and Jim Belasco for their love, support and friendship over many years. Thomas Oglesby, who went over every word several times, to make sure the stanzas of poems broke with the precise meaning I intended. The encouraging words of endorsement from Arnold Palmer, Ken Blanchard, Rabbi Telushkin and Lisa Nichols carry great meaning for me and I thank each of you from the bottom of my heart.

As you read through my collection of poetry, I hope it might inspire you to connect to similar moments in your life and provide a framework for you to think through your own travels in love and life. Though we often look to others for our own inner peace and happiness, it is only through truly loving ourselves and those around us that we can discover the ultimate purpose in life: to grow our souls.

I enjoy hearing from people who read my poems and who let me know which stanza touched their soul. Please feel free to visit my website at www.RichardJaffe.net and join my loving community.

Richard Jaffe
La Jolla, California
Fall 2007

Table of Contents

Romantic Love

Family Love

Love in Death

Introduction

As a young man in my midtwenties, I fell in love with a beautiful, special young woman. After a long time of seeing each other constantly, it felt as though we were connected as two bodies with only one soul. Together, we explored a universe others only dreamed of and a love so deep and so pure, that if I could have stayed that happy the rest of my life, I certainly would have asked her to marry me.

We danced and we sang and we played, even at a time when I faced serious business challenges. Then, without warning, an awkward space began slowly growing between us. We still loved each other desperately, but something was just not right. Neither of us did anything wrong, our love just ran out of time.

A few days later (which seemed like an eternity) I tried to call her but she would not answer. After several futile attempts, I began to worry about her safety. Then, she finally answered the phone (and later I wished she had not). She explained that she loved me very much but could no longer see me. Neither of us had ever loved so hard for so long, or hurt so deep. Then, without saying another word, she hung up the phone. It was over! I never did get a chance to express how I felt.

I had so much love and emotion bursting inside, I needed to do something to let it out. So I decided to sit

down and write her a poem about how I felt. In the poem "Right There," I shared the thoughts and feelings I had bottled up inside. Though I began writing for her, in the end I knew I was writing for myself. For the next thirty years, I continued to write. I have tried to capture the loves and lessons of my journey through life and death.

I am so blessed to have found a best friend and soul mate in my wife Ann. So many of these poems have been inspired by the love, respect and admiration that I have for her. Each of the poems in this book reflects a special time in my life when I was able to express in words what my heart was feeling.

The poem, "Eternal Happiness" is my philosophy in life. "A Boy Becomes a Man" was written when my best friend's father passed away. "Proposal of Love" is how I proposed to my wife. "My New Born Son" was written when my first child was born. This book of poetry is filled with different lessons for different people.

The chapter **Looking for Love** details my belief that true love is out there even though I couldn't touch it yet. It is almost like I was standing in a silent room with the radio turned off. All I had to do was find the right switch and the sound appeared. Though I couldn't hear it before, the room was always filled with radio waves (and love).

Finding Love expresses all the love, joy, and hope two hearts can feel when we love the other person more than we love ourselves. Each time we feel this powerful emotion, we hope and pray that it will last forever. Even though only one love can possibly last forever, we never prepare ourselves for the day it disappears. **Lost Love** describes the emptiness and loneliness that consumes us after love runs out of time. It seems like time stands still while our heart is breaking on the long walk back to ourselves that we never even dreamed about.

The chapter on **Romantic Love** is written as I look back with fondness on the memories of the young loves in my life that were fresh with infatuation and innocence. Throughout my life I have been loved and supported beyond belief by my family and friends. **Family Love** poems are expressions of appreciation for the loved ones who have continued to love me for who I really am.

Finally, poems in **Love in Death** are inspirations from the lives of people who have touched me deep within my own soul. Though saddened, empty and without explanation of why people died (and often too soon), each separate life already healed their own souls, taught us lessons in life, and gave meaning and feeling to those lives they touched.

Most of us spend our entire lives searching for love in hope of finding a happiness that will last forever. One of the most important lessons I have learned is that

only after we accept that the path to happiness is unveiled through inner peace can we become blessed with a love that brings us eternal happiness. Inner peace is discovered on the journey into our own souls. Acceptance of who we really are and a happiness with one's own true self frees us from worrying about judgment from other people and even ourselves. When we truly love ourselves and become our own best friend (not an easy bond to make), we begin attracting love and energy that radiates an inner peace that others yearn to be around.

I hope the love, faith and emotions I share through my poems will give you direction, hope, and strength to search your own soul for the inner peace and eternal happiness you so richly deserve.

Richard Jaffe
La Jolla, California
Fall 2007

6

Part One

Looking For Love

Eternal Happiness

Our lifetimes pass so swiftly
In the search for what is real,
It often takes another's heart
To know what we can feel.

And though love's bond with friendship
Is the strongest ever known,
It's inner peace and happiness
We must discover on our own.

For love that brings us happiness
Blinds with strength knowing we are sure,
But what if we awake one day
And that love remains no more?

Our soul will fill with loneliness
And emptiness abound,
We will have lost our happiness
Until another love is found.

But a happiness with one's own true self,
Not an easy bond to make,
Allows our heart to pour out love
Without the need to take.

And then if we be blessed with love
Found only "wished upon a star,"
Do we first begin our journey
In search of who we really are.

So if we find everlasting love,
The one fate has meant to be,
Together, we will inspire Him
To set our spirits free.

But if it's just another love
To teach us how to care,
We each will have our own happiness
And inner peace still left to share.

February 14, 1979

The Butterfly of Love

The path of love is like the beauty of a butterfly
Traveling in effortless motion
At a pace that blurs its hidden beauty.
Only upon discovering just the right time and place
Will she carefully settle down.

Then, if finding complete trust,
She slowly spreads her wings
To reveal such awesome beauty
That even nature's fiery colors
Can only thirst to quench.

Envisioning such beauty, we dream of depths
That only time and nature can provide.
Then, without reason and always too soon,
She lifts up and flutters away,
Leaving in her place a sadness
For the empty space she left behind.

But in truth,
She leaves behind beauty
Which lies deep within our hearts,
And only escapes through the window
Allowing us to see within our souls.

So next time you engage
The stillness of love's butterfly,
Cup your heart a little more gently
And behold the beauty
Of each passing moment.

June 7, 1980

From a Family of Love

From beauty showering the horizon
Where mountains burst into the sky
To the depths of love's emotion
I often question why.

Why should I be so fortunate
To lead a life of love?
Living each day searching inward
For my guiding force above.

For harbored deep beneath my soul
Await journeys only I foresee.
Exploring each new voyage
Reveals greater depths that I love me.

Concealed within my inner peace
Life's true meaning I may know.
Only by sharing love's awareness
Does happiness learn to grow.

I've been blessed with a special family
Whose love grows only from its giving,
Providing me the strength and confidence
To share love every day I'm living.

And when my heart searches outside
Completely naked may it roam,
For if lonely and rejected
I know that love awaits at home.

Each day now I love to live
And live to love as well,
Knowing someday soon within my heart
An even greater love will swell.

Though it's hard for me to imagine
A greater happiness in life,
I know it will keep growing
Until the day I take a wife.

And then our lives begin again,
A new universe to explore.
Two souls sewn together in love and trust
Surpass all happiness before.

But for my present time and space
I share my love in poems,
Forever grateful to my family
Where love has found so many homes.

April 4, 1980

Falling Off a Rainbow

Love is such a potent force
To build our lives around,
It climbs the highest rainbow
Then knocks us to the ground.

For nowhere is it written
That the laws of love are fair,
Injecting hearts with ecstasy
Then draining with despair.

Though living without loving
May seem such a shallow place,
Living after loving ends
Is the deepest hurt to face.

When tenderness and laughter
That sets true love apart
Deflates to sudden loneliness
Of an empty, aching heart.

The time has come to search our souls
And seek happiness from within,
To provide the strength to stand alone
Until a new love does begin.

So while empty and still wanting,
Love remains life's greatest pleasure,
Unveiling depths of happiness
We never learn to measure.

And as the evening sky grows dark
Without love's gentle care,
Remember, it must always storm
For a rainbow to appear!

June 21,1981

Building Strength in Happiness

How often do I ask myself
Of why He did choose me
To live out all the happiness
He ever meant to be.

For all my life's been lucky,
Things always happen for the best.
I merely search for inner peace
And He takes care of all the rest.

But sometimes I do lose the path
Such happiness does bring
When struck by Cupid's arrow
My heart swells from the mortal sting.

No longer alone with my own destiny
An outside force is brought within,
Only by learning how to sacrifice
Do I discover places I've not been.

Because when I am alone in love
Though contentment does exist,
Without attraction to another soul
So much of love is missed.

Like sharing joys of laughter
That a fresh new heart may bring,
Or finding out the little things
That make my spirit sing.

Or learning of the tenderness
Only a woman can uncover,
To grow happiness within my friendship
Requires much more than just a lover.

I need to find another soul
Who knows the pleasures found in giving
And who appreciates the specialness
To share love every day we're living.

But even when I meet with love
Whose treasures I desperately yearn to keep,
By remaining within my own happiness
Will my path never climb too steep.

For just the nature of love's mystery
Means sharing all the good times with the bad
And many secrets of happiness
Come from lessons learned while sad.

So while love's passion shall soon strike me
A willing target I remain,
For now I'm building strength in happiness
To withstand the days that love brings pain.

July 13, 1980

Tapestry of Life

Life is a multicolored tapestry
We weave through heartaches and rejoices.
It vibrates from the fabric of our morals
While reflecting the wisdom of our choices.

Though most of us spend our lifetimes
Chasing love, our ultimate goal,
The path to inner peace and happiness
Is revealed by learning to grow our soul.

For each love in life is a precious thread
With new lessons we must share
Colored with lasting memories
That teach love's greatest gift,
Learning how to care.

But another's love is not the path
We must explore to find life's purpose.
When looking to others for our answers
We only find their questions on the surface.

We must search within our own hearts
To love the only soul we see.
Acceptance of who we are today
Is the first step to becoming who we want to be.

Because life is all about our attitudes
And the point of view we choose to take,
Accepting the things we cannot change
While taking responsibility for choices that we make.

For once we love our own soul
As much as the one we desperately hope to find,
We build the inner strength and confidence
That leaves empty loneliness behind.

November 13, 1998

Garden of Love

I know you're out there somewhere
In this crazy world of ours,
Either hiding in the bushes
Or dancing with the flowers

That pave my road to happiness
Alongside a separate path for you
To escort me to a universe
Waiting especially for two.

Where tenderness stretches boundaries
A loving touch can show
And inner peace explores the depth
A life of love may know.

For hand in hand we'll travel
To share both the pleasures and pain
And build our strength from happiness
To see sunshine through the rain.

So do not stop your dancing yet
To look where I may be,
Just play within your garden
And let your spirit roam carefree.

When the time is perfect
For our paths of life to meet,
There still remains a lifetime
To be swept up off our feet.

November 17, 1980

Gentle as a Heartbeat

My tenderness is an expression
Of just how deeply I have touched
My own soul.

Quietly, and with patience,
I can feel from where my own heart beats.
And, should I open my arms up to you,
Come lie beside me and listen!

Only when you can feel a quietness flow from within
Can we reach out and touch with a tenderness
As gentle as a heartbeat.

July, 1979

Spiritual Love

I seem to have discovered how to explore
The innermost depths of my own happiness.
It can be done with
The awareness and appreciation for the beloved.

I can transcend the physical love
To a level where two spirits touch
And continue to grow
Where words have no meaning
And even physical presence is no longer necessary.

April 4, 1980

26

Part Two

Found Love

Proposal of Love

While life consumes our mortal souls
First spank till final death,
Our spirits search for happiness
Beyond our final breath.

Already our days are numbered
That we walk upon this earth
But forever has no boundaries,
Just a beginning we call birth.

While exploring life's true meaning
Our hearts fell helplessly in love,
Like two feathers floating freely
With His guiding force above.

But once our separate paths engaged
The outcome left no doubt,
We've only just begun to learn
What eternal love's about.

Deep beneath the solitude
Our inner peace reveals,
Lie depths of endless happiness
Two hearts in love can feel.

And never have I met someone
Whose soul's so pure and sweet,
Through laughter, trust and tenderness
You fulfill my needs complete.

My heart aches when I'm without you
But a moment or a day,
I need to live my life with you
In love and health, I pray.

You are who I've dreamt about
To share my family and life,
With all my love, I ask you, Dear,
Will you forever be my wife?

June 16, 1984

Eternal Friendship

As we stand beneath the chupah
Forever endlessly in love,
I give thanks to God Almighty
Who guides our fate from high above.

In you I've found my perfect twin
To share all my hopes and dreams.
With your strength and sensitivity,
We make the perfect team.

We are so very fortunate
To have been raised in such loving homes,
Teaching respect, care and honesty
You've captured deep within your poems.

Ever since our paths engaged
My heart aches to join as one.
I need to spend my life with you
Till all our days are done.

Only by teaching our children to understand
Shabbat, tzedakah, and shalom,
We'll weave the threads of our heritage
To build our Jewish home.

But today our lives begin anew,
Just you and me alone
Entering the bonds of eternal friendship,
The strongest happiness ever known.

For you are who I've dreamt about
To share my family and life.
With all my love, I answer, Dear,
Yes, I will forever be your wife.

Ann Levinson Jaffe
Richard Jaffe
December 8, 1984

Everlasting Friendship

From somewhere high above the heavens
A stray arrow pierced my heart,
Shattering the stillness of my peaceful soul
And exposing naked emotions from the start.

With a hunger, lust and passion
I had never felt so deep,
Our bodies ached to join together
When apart our souls would weep.

It appeared without a warning
So sudden and so strong,
With the fire of pure emotion.
To whom did my heart belong?

Your eyes sparkled with desire,
Your kisses wet and hot and sweet,
Your touch, your smile, your everything,
Sparked my passion so complete.

But I have already made commitments
That are sacred and run deep,
While your soul searches on its journey
You have your own destiny to keep.

For our friendship to last forever
Will take wisdom, luck and caring.
I know your loyalty is unending
With no boundaries to your sharing.

But if you can learn to love yourself
The way that you love me,
Your soul will find an inner peace
And a best friend for eternity.

July 27,1982

My Perfect Twin

If I could dream my perfect twin
To share life's destiny,
Her warmth and sensitivity
Would set my spirit free.

She'd be strong and confident
With a peaceful soul to share,
Embodied with fiery compassion
Expressing love and trust and care.

Love without expression
Is like a flower before the bloom,
A caterpillar not yet a butterfly,
A child still inside the womb.

Though feeling love is wonderful,
The greatest pleasure known while living,
Life's greatest lesson ever learned
Is the gift of love is giving.

Yet love is not a lesson
To be taught within a poem,
But rather deep emotions
Best learned within a giving home.

Growing up with loving parents
One learns lessons we can't teach,
That love has endless boundaries
With depths only giving love can reach.

Children love to imitate
What parents mostly show.
When raised with constant love and praise,
It's confidence we learn to grow.

I won't need to teach my twin
The secret of love and happiness,
Already she will know the path
Of giving love will lead to bliss.

While others search the universe
To make their spirits whole,
I turn my own eyes inward
And explore new depths of my own soul.

For I no longer need to find
"My perfect twin" in life.
I found that special lady
The day you said you'd be my wife.

July 10, 1989

"Joie de Vivre" (Love of Life)

Your eyes sparkle with a magnificence
As none I've ever known,
They radiate a warmth and joy
A beauty all their own.

Yet deep within the caverns
From whence these eyes do peer,
There lies a gentle, little girl
Whose voice I think I hear.

Silently she cries out for a man
And the strength he can provide,
To light the spark, make a woman glow
From her own specialness inside.

Somehow I have found the match
That sets my own fire burning.
Through trust and love and inner peace
Life's happiness I am learning.

Together with my candle
And the experiences I've been through,
I wish to shine a guiding light
On a peace that's right for you.

Still, you alone must search your soul
To find the love you bear within.
I can merely wait and hope
And point where you might begin.

If fate should come to bless us,
Exchange trust and love as well,
No boundaries have our friendship
Only passing time will tell.

But if by chance our lives fail to mix
And find the time to share,
Already you have fueled my flame
And made me more aware.

December 6, 1978

The Passion of Your Presence

I looked up and in an instant
My body shuddered with a jolt,
A breathless, tingling energy
Pierced through me like a lightning bolt.

My heart pounded with desire
At your beauty so intense,
But it wasn't till our eyes first kissed
I felt the passion of your presence.

A stranger just a moment past,
Future soulmates almost certain
Your smile burst into my wildest dreams,
My heart danced while yours kept flirtin'.

Where did this magic come from?
Who sent you, for how long?
Were our paths in life predestined
To write lyrics for a new love song?

Then for just an instant
I panicked, did you too feel this glow?
But just as swiftly did I realize
A flower needs the sun to grow.

Tasting sweeter than the first spring day
Time stood still, but no longer whole.
As I reached out to touch my empty heart
Your smile soothed my aching soul.

December 18, 1992

Best of Friends Forever

Our lives are drawn together
By a guiding force above,
Even angels' voices quiver
At such passion and such love.

For so powerful is our attraction
Like a caged eagle once set free,
Soaring far beyond the horizon
Our souls have met their destiny.

As each day unveils new happiness
My heart beckons, "Can this love be true?"
I have waited my whole lifetime
To meet a soulmate just like you.

With your beauty, strength and honesty
We've created heaven here on earth,
Exploring the depths of love and friendship
I've been searching for since birth.

My heart aches when I'm without you
But a moment or a day,
I need your love to shine inside me
For my soul to see its way.

I've grown desperate for your gentle touch
Whether together or apart,
Each day I wake to feel the tenderness
Of your pure and perfect heart.

So every day I say I love you
I'm filled with passion and a tear.
I cry with longing when I'm without you,
I cry with joy when you are near.

Our lives are blessed with awesome love
Whose bonds are one and cannot sever.
One of Life's truths I know for certain
We are best of friends forever!

June 16, 1994

Two Hearts Just Holding Hands

My heart hungers for the moment
When we can once again embrace,
To feel the passion of your presence,
Taste the beauty of your grace.

You touch the core of my true essence
Awakening emotions I've never known,
Creating a path of love and happiness
To a new universe all our own.

Where our spirits soar like eagles
To explore the origins from whence we came,
I feel like I've been born again
Life will never be the same.

Together we will search the stars
To learn the true purpose of why we're here.
My journey has found a perfect soulmate
With whom to love and laugh and care.

Having tasted the sweet nectar
Of two bodies sharing the same soul,
Each breath bursts with new excitement
Your happiness has become my only goal.

As you caress my naked soul,
Learn to share and touch and listen,
Only through laughter, trust and tenderness
May we grow our happiness from within.

Though we have just begun our journey
Love gives no guarantees.
While we may think we are its masters
We only serve as long as love may please.

While we are blessed to share a sacred bond
Our journey will never be quite done.
My soul cries out to lie beside you,
My heart aches to be as one.

Wherever love may lead us,
I know we're meant to share its plans.
Remember, we will always be connected
Like two hearts just holding hands.

April 19, 2001

Let Me Be Your Angel

As life unfolds before me
I never feel alone,
I'm surrounded by a spirit
Whose face I've never known.
It reaches deep inside me
Beyond the heavens high above.
It shines a guiding light on me
That showers me with love.

I'm not sure when I first noticed,
Like a friend from lifetimes past.
I feel a warmth and peacefulness
Eternal love destined to last.
She is my special angel
Teaching me right from wrong.
I lean upon her gentle shoulder
When I need faith to keep me strong.

It must be hard to be my angel,
Omnipresent and knowing all,
Whispering words of encouragement
Then allowing me to fall.
Already she has taught me
How to listen and to care.
Overflowing with love and passion,
I need another soul to share.

I sensed a rare and sacred bond
The instant our hearts met.
We share a spiritual connection,
The deepest I've felt yet.
I feel your loving presence
Each moment of every day.
I will shine a guiding light on you
In peace and health you'll stay.

Though we have two separate bodies,
We share one eternal soul.
Your inner peace and happiness
Have become my lifetime goal.
Regardless where life leads you,
Even loneliness and despair,
Cry out unto your angel,
My loving touch is always there.

So will you let me be your angel
To share your journey throughout life?
I will celebrate your victories,
And comfort you through strife.
For I am your blessed angel,
Though I may disappear for a while.
Just think of me, I'll be hiding
Within the happiness of your smile.

March 11, 2007

46

Part Three

Lost Love

Right There

We caught something very special
A love that can't compare
To the feelings I've experienced
Anytime, anyplace, anywhere.

Your beauty, wit and goodness
Are something very rare,
But that's only a small part of what
Makes us a special pair.

It would be great to travel
Life's rugged path as two,
Always together sharing
With someone as nice as you.

But there still remain too many
Of life's lessons left unlearned,
So we must journey onward,
Take the risk we might get burned.

It's hard to understand inside
That though we still do care,
Our paths cannot exactly match
And sometimes they will veer.

It's only for a short time now,
To make us more aware
Of what we each possess inside,
To know what we can share.

To hurdle this strange distance
Which we can't deny is there
Is to strengthen our bond together
To a point which cannot tear.

Yet if we've reached a place too deep
Which puts us beyond repair,
I will look at what we've gained, not lost,
And fight to hold back the tears.

I have no easy answers
To what we must face here,
I only have my love for you
And my deepest prayer.

Let us be strong and confident,
Give our best shot if we dare.
I know that if we get the chance
We'll find ourselves "right there."

February 11, 1978

Happiness in Love

I feel a fire burning
Deep within my soul,
I give it no direction
For it has no final goal.

It makes me tingle, feel alive,
It's wonderful to care.
Matters not if I am all alone
Or two as in a pair.

My emotions are reflections of
Who I am and where I've been.
It teaches me life's purpose is
To love, not who will win.

This flame that glows comes from within
A place I know not where,
A special, cozy, inner peace,
A confidence to share.

Naked are my emotions,
No shelter, I am bare.
But that's the only meeting place
Two hearts can honestly share.

I have my faults, and you have yours,
We're only human too
I ask not for forgiveness
I am me and you are you.

Respect for our differences
Will keep our fires strong
Though we may think we're always right,
Sometimes we know we're wrong.

No matter where life leads us,
Our flames we must keep burning.
To find the strength we possess inside
Requires never ending learning.

I wish for you, like all mankind,
A happiness abound,
An inner peace, a gratitude
For loved ones still around.

While some search for life's true meaning
In the stars that lie above,
I turn my own eyes inward,
And find happiness in love.

February 12, 1978

Reflecting in Love's Aftermath

Reflecting in love's aftermath
Is an experience in appreciation
For the wonders of love's gift.
It is a time to collect all the lessons and memories,
Even the ones taken for granted
Till they remain no more.

Though I feel a sadness
For the empty space inside me,
I feel a certain kind of strength,
A confidence,
As I slowly fill that gap with my own self.

I know the last time I felt this gap,
It was so much smaller!
This time, it was stretched to places
I never dreamed of reaching.

I took control
And dared love to take me to its limit!
Never once considering
That on the long walk back to myself,
I would be traveling alone.

March 2, 1978

Time to Love Again

Life was so easy then,
Even in the hardest times.
The sun shined through my smile
And the stars sparkled in my eyes.

There was no such thing as reaching too far,
All I had to do was reach
And it was mine.

And so, when I ask myself
Why love must disappear
Just when I'm getting used to having it around,
I already know.

For even now
As I begin to fill that void,
I know that someday soon
The sides will be overflowing,
Too small for even my own self
To fit into.

Only then will it be time
To love again.

March 2, 1978

Through Memories of Love

Love is such a pretty place
With flowers everywhere,
Through open arms and warm embrace
We show how much we care.

By merely sharing presence
Love grows within the space,
Outside my heart, within my touch,
A very special place.

Feelings journey deeper
Than words could ever know.
They tap a source of strength within
Impossible to show.

For deep within my friendship
Grows the strength that love can bring,
To share a joy and happiness
That makes my spirit sing.

Yet when comes the time to separate
It's the memories of love
That feed my soul, and burst my heart
To places far above.

For though love's greatest pleasure
Is the ability to share,
To measure my own happiness
Demands no one else be there.

Once alone within my soul
There is no place to hide,
Where love and happiness learn to co-exist
They travel side by side.

Though I treasure all the moments
We've shared together, and alone,
Words fail to resonate the magnitude
My feelings since have grown.

As I continue on life's journey
Love grows within my space,
And deep within my own happiness
Your love holds such a special place.

October 28, 1979

Love's Separate Halves

Memories still linger
Of a place our hearts once shared
Outside this very universe
Alone together, nothing else compared.

Now time has injected a distance
As our lives take different paths.
Our souls need different meaning,
No longer whole but separate halves.

Your friendship means too much to me
To ever let stop growing,
Without an occasional visit
We may drift apart, without even knowing.

Let's show some perseverance
Though we're both busy as can be
Let's set a date, a place, a time,
For dinner, you and me.

The past is well behind us now,
The present stares us in the eye.
Love came and went, always to remain
I'll never question why.

June 10, 1978

The Knife of Disappointment

Disappointment is such an empty feeling.
Not lonely,
For loneliness merely begs for company.

But rather a rude awakening
That expectations and aspirations
Were removed from the truth.

The knife cuts deepest
Not because someone failed to act as desired,
But rather in oneself for allowing
Such dreams to surface
Without ever looking for actions
To support promising words.

Or were words spoken really true,
Only I found meaning a sensitive heart longed to uncover?

May 9, 1980

Come Touch With Us

Without a storm is raging
Mother nature spreads her wings
Within my heart is burning,
Filled with peace and love it sings.

It doesn't take a night like this
To make me more aware,
But honesty with my own emotions
And good friends with whom to share.

Yet we all must face the heartbreak,
A lover disappears, we're left alone.
It is then we must look inward
To find the happiness love has sown.

So if you're down and lonely
Without another over which to fuss,
Just open your heart, extend your hand
And come touch with the rest of us.

January 24, 1979

Part Four

Romantic Love

The Bubble of Ecstasy

We met as friends from college days
Though strangers we really be,
Yet we somehow touched upon the spark
That set our spirits free.

Enormous energies surrounded us
Whose source we know not where,
Discovering the "bubble of ecstasy"
Often sought, but found so rare.

We spent the night together
Only our bodies kept us apart.
My heart was light, your mouth so warm
We felt it was just the start.

Though for two weeks hence we parted
Your touch completely filled my soul.
While business occupied my mind
Your heart remained my only goal.

I packed my bags to journey
To a niche that you call home,
To touch and hold and cuddle up
And let our spirits roam.

My ride was filled with visions
Where my heart always wished to be.
It made me feel alive again,
So glad that I am me.

And when I saw your face again
You snuggled close beneath my chin.
I felt our bubble stretch itself
To places I had never been.

All night our bubble soared in leaps and bounds
Quite a reckless pace to grow.
We gave no thoughts to what might later be
Or that maybe we should slow.

Then suddenly it happened
Our bubble burst into thin air.
All the energy surrounding us
Just seemed to disappear.

Though filled with disappointment
There was a lesson to be learned:
Through patience and understanding
Love requires more concern.

And though our bubble vanished
As quickly as it first appeared,
It's better to have loved and lost
Than never to have cared.

August 7, 1979

Teenage Love

When I was young and quite naive
In what love would later bring,
I met a rare and special friend
Who made my spirit sing.

At first our hearts were distant
Many friends lay in between
But passing time and shared experiences
Cast a light few had ever seen.

Though her eyes were so inviting
Was not her beauty that drew me near,
But rather a quiet confidence
We both knew we would share.

So daily we grew closer
Sharing tears and laughs and hurts,
Until one day it happened
Into love our friendship burst.

Each minute held new meaning
As so quickly each day passed,
For soon I'd leave for college
Somehow we knew it couldn't last.

Living for the moment
We tasted what love and life's about,
Touching deep within another's heart
Was our lesson there's no doubt.

And as our love did slowly fade away
Our friendship still remained.
Instead of losing a treasured lover,
An even closer friend I gained.

Her smile, warmth and loving touch
Were carried everywhere I went,
I never lost the memory
Of those fun-filled days we spent.

Now as months stretch into years
And to each our separate ways,
My thoughts do wander back to her
And where now her spirit lays.

June 11, 1979

The Spark of Specialness

We met upon an island
Beneath the sun and near the sea.
The vacation seemed like paradise,
Everything so heavenly.

I had filled six lovely days
One more till my journey home
And you arrived the night before,
A full week left to roam.

Yet somehow in our passing streams
A spark caught and filled the air,
Excitement burst, affection flowed,
I just had to hold you near.

When far from home and time is short
Who questions what is real,
We danced until the sunrise
Everything seemed so surreal.

For sometimes on vacation
A new lover one may meet,
But when returning to reality
The fruit doesn't taste as sweet.

So down to Brooklyn Heights I drove
To touch the truth, I had to know
If our seedling harbored all the energy
A young flower needs to grow.

Two weeks faded images
Of how you did appear,
Yet I sensed a flow of energy
As our outstretched hands came near.

The precious hours flew by
Filled with wine and idle chatter.
We even strolled the promenade,
Sharing time was all that mattered.

As our conversation rambled on,
I knew things had changed, they always do,
Yet deep beneath a new environment
I was still me and you were you.

Any doubts I had envisioned
Disappeared as night turned into day.
Our closeness kept on growing.
When I left, I wished to stay.

January 9, 1979

Reunion Romance

The evening echoed memories
Reunions often bring.
My heart rejoiced with happiness,
Old friendships learned to sing.

When late at night it happened
Our hearts burst upon first glance
And scattered seeds of happiness
Throughout the garden of romance.

Sudden energies uplifted us,
We soared high into the clouds.
Her words, like music to my ears,
Sang far above the crowds.

Somehow we had captured
The spark that draws two spirits near.
I sensed a strength of happiness
Whose source I wished to share.

With beauty, warmth, and wisdom
Her sparkling eyes caressed my soul,
Arousing dormant energy
To make my spirit whole.

For I, in turn, possess within
New depths of love untold,
Where secrets to my happiness
In life and love unfold.

Only passing time will tell
What fate might have in store,
If merely bonds of friendship
Or a depth to share much more.

For already she has shown me
Consideration grows within her heart,
The only seed of energy
My friendship needs to start.

December 23,1982

Toots

The years have flown right by us
Since the days our hearts were one,
Yet time and other lovers
Cannot fog memories of all our fun.

We were young and carefree,
The old college days, you know,
I had my house, my heart, your hand
And dreams to help us grow.

Then as fate would have it
Our paths went separate ways.
I learned of love and happiness
That would return in future days.

Years and lovers later
A fondness still remains
For that crazy, giggly little girl
I was never sure was sane.

Still, I will look through clouded eyes
When your memories come to mind.
It's peace and health and happiness
I hope you'll always find.

October 17, 1978

Mystery Lady

A glance

A spark

A smile

A ttraction

A ffection

A ?

April 6, 1979

Changing Nests

A woman's true colors
Are always seen best
When her feathers are ruffled
While changing her nest.

Yet if she can keep
A smile that glows
Her happiness transcends
All the beauty she shows.

April 22, 1980

Part Five

Family Love

Just You and Me

The precious days are numbered
That we share this life alone,
For soon our seed of love will sprout
A new life of its own.

And though we feel so ready
For our first child to appear,
Oh, how I've loved the silence
With quiet romance in the air.

But ever since the day we met
Eternal love has blessed my soul.
To express my love and inner peace
Has become a lifetime goal.

Though I've tried by writing poetry
And whispered tenderly, "I care,"
My words can only long to touch
The depths of love we share.

For words will never satisfy
Emotions of the heart,
Nor ease the pain or soothe the ache
Of time we spend apart.

Children and the love they bring
Provide a new universe to explore,
Where souls find true expression
Like love has never known before.

Though I promise to keep writing
Of all the joys children may bring,
Remember, you are the special one
Who always makes my spirit sing.

So let's treasure quiet moments now
We share together while still free,
And paint everlasting memories
Of the days "JUST YOU AND ME."

August 31, 1986

My Newborn Son

Today is your Bris, my newborn son.
The miracle of life has only begun.
Though the Mohel may cut outer flesh and take skin,
Happiness in life resides deep within.

Already you're blessed with my very first goal:
A healthy body, sound mind, and a pure, peaceful soul.
As destiny beckons you to come forth and share,
Challenge yourself to be as great as you dare.

For I'll always be there with a supporting hand.
When you stumble and fall, I'll help you to stand.
My father taught me to be successful in life
By confronting adversity and conquering strife.

But the ultimate person you grow up to be
Depends on your choices and not upon me.
So when it's your turn to stand on your own
Remember I love you, you're never alone.

As you travel life's journey and search high above,
Turn your eyes inward and express all your love.
You are a leader, compassionate and strong.
Trust your own instincts and you will never go wrong.
When you don't worry what others believe
No limits exist to what you may achieve.

If you select building castles of wealth
Remember your loved ones, your morals, your health.
If inner peace is your ultimate goal,
Its secret is waiting within your own soul.

Whatever you choose I'll be there to share,
To love and to cherish, to show that I care.
I'll always provide you a wise guiding hand
Like Moses, who led our people to the promised land.

Life is the journey to who you will be.
Only you are the author to your own destiny.
Today, I thank God, his greatest miracle well done,
For health and Shalom for my dear newborn son.

March 13, 1987

My Son and Me

Before dawn has even broken
To wipe daylight from her eyes,
Our bedroom door creaks open
As my son beckons me to rise.

Though my body aches for one more moment
To rest my weary bones,
I hear a quiet serenade.
"Eyes open daddy" his voice moans.

As I lie in bed pretending
I've not awakened from my sleep,
His persistence knows no boundaries
Only it's playtime I must keep.

For early morning is our private time
We talk and eat and play,
Rejoicing life's most precious gift
To share love and health each day.

So as he pulls off all my covers
Excitement dances on his face
While my wife grins a loving smile
She rolls over in my place.

Then suddenly he leaps into my arms,
His favorite place to be.
My heart bursts with pride and endless love
Knowing his soul is really part of me.

Though exhausted and quite early
There's no place else I'd rather be.
I'll never trade those precious moments
Together, just my Son and Me.

October 17, 1989

Love for a Daughter

My life is blessed with many loves
That fuel my soul to grow,
But there's something special about a daughter's smile
That stirs my emotions deep below.

Her eyes sparkle with a beauty
That truly takes my breath away
When I look into those big brown eyes
Her soul begs my heart to stay.

For her time has no finite boundaries
A lifetime will never be enough
To share the joys and happy mitzvahs
As well as tears when times get tough.

Though my journey's had peaks and valleys
Teaching new lessons all the time,
How I want her to see from my mountain tops
And hear stories of my climb.

We will always walk and talk together,
Hand in hand we'll take our strolls,
Exploring life's road to happiness,
Reaching each our separate goals.

For the essence of humanity
Is raising children happy and carefree.
I know I'll find no greater love
Than for my daughter, sweet Charly.

March 11, 1990

Unconditional Love

My life is blessed with so much love,
Good fortune shines everywhere I turn.
My soul aches to search the universe.
I still have so much more to learn.

Yet each day I wake to face the challenge
Of how to divide my time and attention.
Without nurturing my own need for solitude
My inner peace fills with stress and tension.

But I have found a secret resting place
To visit whenever life gets tough,
That unwinds my mind and soothes my soul
Where love's passion never grows enough.

I merely dream of the special family
I am blessed with here on earth,
My soul mate wife and loving kids,
Especially the miracle of each daughter's birth.

Filled with tears of awe and gratitude
I hold her new life oh so near.
With a heart and soul so perfect,
She radiates complete trust without a fear.

For to her love has no boundaries
Only endless depth to share
Not asking for commitment,
Rather just another soul to care.

As she grows from birth through teenage years
At times we'll disagree what is best.
With our bonds of love and friendship
We will mend each and every test.

Only through the lessons of her lifetime
Will she weave a character all her own,
Demanding respect and independence
From the fabric of values already sewn.

Yet as I gaze into her sparkling eyes
That just melt my heart away,
My soul bursts with pride and happiness
To share such nachas here today.

Already she has taught me
To pause and thank the Lord above
For the blessing of Birth's greatest gift:
A daughter's unconditional love.

May 1, 1993

My Bar Mitzvah Son

Today is your Bar Mitzvah
My handsome, precious son.
Your lifelong Jewish journey
Has only just begun.

While the legacy of our ancestors
Conquered adversity and strife,
As a son of the Commandments,
Walk a holy path through life.

For you are a kind and gentle leader
Like many of your forefathers in the past.
As an adult in the Jewish community,
Give back something that will last.

While Tikkun Olam, to repair the world
Is a responsibility we all share,
Challenge yourself to do good deeds
Just to show how much you care.

Success in life is not measured
By what you end up with for yourself,
Rather through acts of Mitzvahs and Tzedakah
Do you create a spiritual wealth.

As you search for life's true meaning
Use Jewish values as your guide,
Treat everyone with care and respect
To find where peace and love reside.

If you forget your Jewish values
And harbor thoughts of self and greed,
Your life will be like an empty Mezuzah,
A hollow shell without a spiritual seed.

When you live a just and righteous life
Learning becomes a lifetime goal,
Through Torah and Jewish studies
You reveal the essence of your soul.

From the moment of your first breath
I've dreamt of sharing this special day.
Your whole life has been a blessing
I thank God each time I pray.

Feel the love we share today
As my heart bursts with gratitude and pride,
No greater gift in life could you have given me, son,
Than to have you, my hero, at my side.
I love you!

March 11, 2000

A Daughter's Bat Mitzvah Day

Today is your Bat Mitzvah,
My precious, darling soul.
From the first day of your blessed life
You've been walking toward this goal.

Though I've tried my best to teach you
Life's lessons that I've learned,
Your wisdom and compassion
Come from lessons that you've earned.

You possess a very special gift
That others long to share.
Your spirit reaches beyond your years,
Your heart shows how much you care.

For you are a gifted leader
People follow and listen to.
Your strength transcends your beauty,
Your love is deep and true.

But today is a new beginning,
The start of your adult Jewish life.
Remember your values and your morals
Through life's adversity and strife.

For we are the chosen people
With responsibilities to fulfill,
Tikkun Olam, to repair the world
Is our eternal mission still.

So choose to walk a holy path
As you explore your lifetime goal,
Embrace Torah, passion and learning
As you unveil your Jewish soul.

Today I thank God deeply
For his divine blessings from above,
For my daughter's special friendship
And her unconditional love.

March 8, 2003

My Darling Bat Mitzvah Girl

Today is your Bat Mitzvah,
My darling little girl.
Your life has been a blessing
More precious than a diamond or a pearl.

From the instant that I saw your face
At the moment of your birth,
I thanked God above the heavens
For sending us an angel here on earth.

Your soul is pure and caring,
You are kind to everyone you meet.
You adore every living animal
You even stop and coo right on the street!

You are happy and quite funny,
Just a pure joy to be around.
Your carefree laugh is so infectious,
The most positive child ever found.

While smart, creative and solution-oriented
No challenge is ever beyond your reach,
Quite self sufficient and so capable
Your strong sense of self no one can teach.

Today you start your Jewish adulthood.
Remember to always act with dignity and grace.
Tikkun Olam is all of our responsibilities,
To make the world a better place.

You are a kind and gentle leader
Like many of your forefathers in the past.
As an adult in the Jewish community
Learn to give back something that will last.

I hope you find a burning passion
That has Jewish learning as its seed,
One you can share with the entire community
That fills a burning, desperate need.

Life is but a journey
Of souls searching to connect.
Through love, trust and compassion
Your life will have a powerful effect.

Be true to all your values,
Live life as a courteous, observant Jew.
Your family is always here to support you
And remember how much "I love you!"

March 4, 2006

Graduating Love

I feel a special gratitude
That life has made us friends.
To share respect and admiration
Provides a love that has no end.

Words will never recognize
That our friendship has no peer.
Within our hearts we understand
The depth of love we share.

You mean so much more than cousin,
And more than brother, too.
For the special gift of caring
Glows from deep inside of you.

As you brighten up the spirits
Of all the lives you touch each day,
You radiate a warmth and joy
In your own very special way.

Though the miles keep us separate
The years continue to draw us near.
Your love and inspiration
Touch me deep and dear.

As you stand up proud today
And touch love and life in part,
Just listen to me applauding
From deep within your heart.

May 25, 1980

Brother Jack

We've shared our lives together
From childhood till now.
Though competing through adolescence
We've grown closer still somehow.

But for you it's been a struggle
To build the confidence you need
As the footsteps you've been following
Are different than the ones you lead.

Older and much wiser now
You've learned to travel your own way
As life demands of each of us
Quite different dues to pay.

Though struggling with adversity
Makes finding happiness much tougher,
Without such a loving family
The road would be so much rougher.

Though your outside has been hardened
By the void disappointment grows,
Inside you've built a heart of gold
Just impossible to know.

For to share within your friendship
Means no boundaries have your giving
As you would gladly sacrifice your safety
To insure that I keep living.

Though words could never capture
All the feelings that we hold,
Within our hearts we understand
The depth of love untold.

When confronted with your loneliness
And search for the inner peace you lack,
Remember, it's forever
That I love you, Brother Jack!

January 10, 1981

Mom and Dad

There are no two people anywhere
Whose love we want more to share,
Whose happiness overflows its bounds
You've taught us how to care.

We've learned to love you more each day
From within the happiness we have grown,
It's easy to love ourselves more each day
With the patience you two have shown.

We could never even repay in part
The love we possess within our hearts,
But every day that we are blessed to share
We'll try our best to start.

You are two very special human beings apart,
Together, an awesome pair.
We dream of a love for ourselves one day
In the same universe you two share.

Wherever life shall lead us now
We go with strength free from any fear,
You've taught us of love and happiness
And to express how much we care.

November 1981

Part Six

Love in Death

A Boy Becomes a Man

A special kind of love attracts
A father and a son.
To share the wisdom of experience
Is a task that's never done.

From the moment we can crawl about
He teaches us to stand.
For the rest of life he's behind us
To provide a guiding hand.

For those of us so lucky
To work together and to share,
There grows a respect and admiration
No other love can quite compare.

For side by side we struggle
To build security and wealth,
Always remembering life's road to happiness
Must be filled with love and health.

Yet one day it must happen
That a father pass away,
And though his presence on earth is gone
His guiding hand will always stay.

Already he has taught us
Of the courage to be strong
And how to stand for what we believe
Though sometimes we'll be wrong.

So when you face adversity,
Search for strength to make you bolder,
Reflect upon the guiding force
Whose hand rests upon your shoulder.

For on the day your father died
A new stage of life began
Because on that very same mournful day
A BOY BECAME A MAN

January 12, 1980

Half a Soul

Our love is etched in detail
Inside my broken heart.
Exploring life and happiness,
I thought we'd never part.

We transcended to a universe
That few have ever known.
While your spirit searches heaven now,
I'm left here all alone.

I know that God creates us
To fulfill a purpose while on earth,
To give ourselves to others
From the instant of our birth.

He decides our destiny
Of when our life will end,
Yet he forgot to brace me for the loneliness
Of losing my best friend.

I'm left with only half a soul,
I know not where to turn.
Though loved ones try to comfort me
The pain and hurt still burn.

You were the very reason
I woke up to greet the day,
Whenever lost or lonely
You would always point the way.

I know not how I will make it
Without you at my side,
My grief is so unbearable,
I want to run away and hide.

Somehow I will search my soul
To find the strength within,
To pick up all the pieces
For my new life to begin.

But know that every waking moment
You're with me in a special way.
Your touch and loving memories
Will never fade away.

February 12, 1989

The Sudden Loss of a Young Loved One

The sudden loss of a young loved one
Makes us stop and question why
We must suffer life's unfairness
First to love, then lose and cry.

Through growing up together
Two spirits often touch as one.
To share the love of friendship
Is a joy surpassed by none.

So though he's gone forever
It's his love he's left behind
To carry deep within your heart
And share what you may find.

So stop to contemplate a while
On those feelings you still share,
Then slowly wake, life carries on,
Still sad, yet more aware.

July 4, 1979

Everlasting Love

It is only through deeds of sacrifice
For those we dearly love
That we discover an untapped source of strength
From a spirit high above.

His memory still cries out
As if always to remind
That though his time on earth has passed
It is his love he's left behind.

Even though you are empty
With a sadness all your own,
Remembering all his love for you
Means you will never be alone.

Take this opportunity
To be with him and to cry,
To thank the Lord for the love you shared
And never question "Why?"

November 2, 1978

Loving Memories

Life is such an awesome mystery
Beyond all depths we comprehend,
From the origins of our beginnings
To the reasons it must end.

We can only watch in reverence
At the miracle of birth.
Though we pray for life eternal,
Time is predestined here on earth.

For no one knows the special secret
How certain people reach old age.
Blessed with years of joyful memories,
Their love is impossible to gauge.

While others much less fortunate
Must die well before their prime,
No matter how we live our lives
We must all face death when it's our time.

But the cruelest hurt in living
Is when a baby has to die,
So helpless, young and innocent.
"Take me instead!" we cry.

Though the reasons are not evident
Why God chose such a beautiful, young life,
While your child's soul is resting peacefully
You must handle all the strife.

Yet no matter what the circumstance
No one can ever take the blame,
For fate is God's will in action
Where the outcome will always be the same.

So let go of all those mournful feelings
That you lost your child at the start,
For his soul and loving memories
Still live deep within your heart.

August 18, 1988

Worlds Apart in Love

The moment that a daughter is born
Our world is such a different place.
Filled with giggles, pink and big warm hugs,
Love bursts through the smile upon her face.

From playful late night escapades
When she wakes just to cuddle in our lap
To that proud and tearful graduation day
When she winks and tips her hat,

Her glorious spirit travels inside of us
Every moment of every day.
There never seems to be enough time
Just to hug and love and play.

For all through life she trusts us
To give her strength if she should fall.
While exploring life's lessons of experience
She knows we're there if she should call.

Then one day it happens
A parent's worst fear that changes all of life.
From a happy, busy family
To empty grief and mournful strife.

Somehow in this senseless world
A daughter's life suddenly is ended,
Leaving a stream of crying broken hearts.
No amount of time will ever mend it.

For though her body is no longer with us
Her words keep speaking in our head.
No longer is she life's student
But rather our teacher now instead.

All life's precious lessons
And love we've shared throughout the years
Can be felt within our broken hearts
And seen through all our crying tears.

Although the pain is absolutely unbearable
Her love is the only strength to get us through.
Just as we can feel her presence still with us
We know that she still feels our love flowing too.

Though we will miss her more than life itself
Her spirit now soars with God above.
We know our souls are still connected
We are JUST WORLDS APART IN LOVE.

March 30, 1996

A Mother's Tribute

A spiritual bond of love connects
A child and a mother,
To learn her values and compassion
Is a tribute like no other.

From the moment of our first breath
She starts teaching us right from wrong,
For the rest of life she instills in us
The confidence to know that we belong.

No one else quite believes in us
In such a blind and passionate way,
Whose trust and endless sacrifice
Continue each and every day.

When we dare to stray beyond the truth
She confronts us to our face,
Always teaching life's true purpose
With such dignity and grace.

Yet one day it must happen
That her time on earth does end.
As her spirit soars unto the heavens,
We cry we've lost our closest friend.

Already she has taught us
The depths of love and eternal hope.
Our souls ache with hollow emptiness
As we search for strength from whence to cope.

While you struggle with your loneliness
Only time can mend your broken heart,
While remembering her compassion
A new stage of life must start.

As you search for life's new meaning
Reflect upon her spirit high above,
Feel her strength grow within your loneliness,
Filling your empty soul with all her love.

For on the day your mother died
Though a part of you died too,
Remember, your lifetime is a tribute
To her lessons and to you.

December 18, 1994

About the Author

Richard Jaffe has written poetry for over three decades, but is most recognized for being a successful entrepreneur and generous philanthropist. **Inner Peace and Happiness:** ***Reflections To Grow Your Soul*** is his first book of published poetry.

In 1975, Richard started Nutri-Foods International Inc., a company that manufactured and distributed Guido's Italian Ices and frozen juice bars. After struggling for many years, Richard turned the company around, took the company public in 1984 and eventually sold it to The Coca Cola Company in 1985 where he renamed the product "Minute Maid Fruit Juicees." After the acquisition, Mr. Jaffe remained President of Nutri-Foods and served on the executive operating committee of The Coca-Cola Foods Division.

The future looked very promising, with the company doubling revenues and with a no-calorie juice bar as well as a Coca Cola sparkling juice bar under development. Midway through his second year, Richard was summoned to Coca Cola's corporate headquarters in Atlanta where he was told to slow down growth and simply maintain the business for two years while executives tried to fix growth problems at Coca Cola Foods. Richard told Chairman Roberto Goizueta that if he couldn't grow the business, he couldn't breathe. They agreed that he would leave the company after completing his second year to find another business he could grow.

Richard was thirty-four years of age when he left Coca Cola. "I decided to take a year off to continue writing poetry and to learn to play golf. After two months, I was itching for something to do and after three months, I needed people around me and a business to grow," said Richard. Lucky, as he usually is, opportunity found Richard. In early 1988, through an acquaintance of his father, Richard was contacted about starting a latex glove company.

"I believe that you create wealth by anticipating future behavior changes and then providing solutions to future needs," said Richard. "I quickly learned that in1987 the Center for Disease Control had issued universal precautions (due to the AIDS crisis) and that all health care workers coming into contact with bodily fluids needed to wear gloves, masks and gowns. So I saw a behavior change: instead of wearing gloves for ten minutes a day, health care workers would wear gloves for ten hours a day. Though I didn't know much about the medical business at the time, I did know how to run a business and how to create customer value," said Richard.

Richard discovered a huge problem: the latex used in making gloves had always been treated with chemicals that if not removed could cause skin rashes if it came in contact with your skin for long periods of time. "What we really needed to do was design a glove that would protect the health care workers from the glove itself," said Richard. His second company, Safeskin, was launched.

In 1989, Safeskin was granted FDA approval to market a hypoallergenic latex exam glove. "We took the approved product and asked our customers: 'how do you like our new gloves and how can we make them better?' They responded, 'could you give us a glove with a little less powder?' What I really heard them say is that they didn't want *any* powder," said Richard. "So the company developed the first hypoallergenic powder-free latex exam glove. Once we introduced it, we knew we had a winner. We ran production twenty-four hours a day, seven days a week, 365 days a year for eight years and couldn't keep up. By 2000, we were making 6.5 billion gloves a year."

Under Richard's leadership, Safeskin went public in 1993, was voted Forbes Magazine's "Best Small Company in America" in 1996, and was purchased by Kimberly-Clark Corporation in 2000. Safeskin continues today as one of the world's most trusted healthcare brands.

After the sale of Safeskin, Richard returned to philanthropy and poetry, but the entrepreneurial spirit struck a third time. In 2006, Richard was introduced to Triosyn, a novel and potentially life-saving antimicrobial technology capable of killing viruses. He recruited several of his former Safeskin executives and created Safe Life Corporation, a medical technology company. They are utilizing the Triosyn technology to commercialize a variety of products beginning with facemasks and respirators, air filtration systems and wound care. In the midst of this third company, Richard has set about to complete a life long goal: the publication of his first book of poetry.

Even through unimaginable adversity and the most challenging times in business, poetry has always provided Richard with a vehicle to express his deepest emotions. "Family and friends are the most important things in life and writing poems to express my love for the people closest to me has allowed me to explore the innermost depths of my own peace and happiness," said Richard. "At the most important occasions in my life (like asking my wife to marry me, the birth of each of my children and the death of someone close to someone I love), poetry has provided me with a tool to express my emotions, keep myself balanced and gain greater perspective on just how lucky I am to have family and friends who truly love me."

Richard is a poet, a seasoned and successful entrepreneur, and a philanthropist. He is also a graduate of Cornell University, where he received a Bachelor of Science degree in Industrial and Labor Relations. Richard resides in La Jolla, CA with his wife Ann and their three children.

To Our Readers

I treasure feedback from those who take the time to read my poetry. I hope to make a difference in people's lives and I hope that my words touch some small part of your life. Please visit me on the web at www.richardjaffe.net. You may also listen to audio versions of my poems, print my poems, and read my favorite quotes. I look forward to hearing from you.

Notes